DONOR BANKS

"Coming!"

DONOR BANKS

SAVING LIVES WITH ORGAN AND TISSUE TRANSPLANTS

SALLY LEE

FRANKLIN WATTS
NEW YORK/LONDON
TORONTO/SYDNEY/1988
A FIRST BOOK

Cover photograph by Paul Liggitt, *San Antonio* Magazine.
Diagrams by Anne Canevari Green.
Cartoon on page 2 courtesy of Rothco.

Photographs courtesy of: Organ Transplantation Program, University
of Texas Health Science Center, San Antonio: pp. 10, 56 (both), 57;
South-Eastern Organ Procurement Foundation: pp. 13, 51; Photo Researchers, Inc.:
pp. 17 (Fawcett), 18 (top—George Whiteley), 18 (bottom—Eric V. Grave), 19
(Arthur Glauberman), 23 (Dr. A. Liepins/Science Photo Library), 32 (top—Jeroboam),
32 (bottom—Biophoto Associates), 33 (Jerome Yeats/Science Photo Library),
34 (CNRI/Science Photo Library), 53 (bottom—Steve Kagan), 58 (bottom—John
Messina); American Association of Blood Banks: pp. 26, 36; South Texas
Regional Blood Bank, San Antonio: p. 28 (both); Taurus Photos: pp. 30
(Laimute E. Druskis), 55 (Martin M. Rotker); Eye Bank at Baptist Medical Center,
San Antonio: pp. 42, 45; The Methodist Hospital—Medical Photography and
Television, Houston, Texas: p. 50; National Kidney Foundation, Inc.: p. 53 (top);
San Antonio Magazine: p. 58 (top-Paul Liggitt); Sally Lee: pp. 66 (both), 67;
National Temporal Bone Banks Program: p. 68; Robert J. Spence, M.D. and The
Maryland Tissue Bank: pp. 73 (both), 74, 75, 85; L. V. Bergman & Assoc., Inc.:
p. 76 (top); Medichrome, Division of The Stock Shop, Inc.: pp. 76 (bottom), 78.

Library of Congress Cataloging-in-Publication Data
Lee, Sally.
Donor banks: saving lives with organ and tissue transplants/by
Sally Lee.
p.   cm. — (A First book)
Includes index.
Summary: Describes the preservation and reuse of eyes, blood, skin
grafts, and hearts through transplant surgery. Also discusses
possible future developments in donor transplants.
ISBN 0-531-10475-3
1. Transplantation of organs, tissues, etc.—Juvenile literature.
2. Preservation of organs, tissues, etc.—Juvenile literature.
3. Tissue banks—Juvenile literature.   [1. Transplantation of
organs, tissues, etc.   2. Preservation of organs, tissues, etc.
3. Tissue banks.]   I. Title.
RD120.76.L44   1988
362.1'783—dc 19   87-27304   CIP   AC

CONTENTS

DONOR BANKS

ONE

STOREHOUSES
OF LIFE

It is still early in the morning, but already the basement of City Hospital is bustling with activity. Glaring lights can be seen through the windows of the operating rooms. Behind each closed door teams of surgeons and nurses work intently to perform the surgery their patients need.

In the first operating room Sara, a young lawyer, lies beneath the bright lights. For years Sara has slowly been going blind. The **cornea,** or clear covering on the front of each eye, has become so cloudy that Sara can see only blurred shapes and shadows. In a delicate operation the eye surgeon is removing the damaged part of one of Sara's corneas and replacing it with healthy tissue. Soon she will be able to see normally out of one eye. Her other eye will receive a new cornea in several months.

Michael, the teenager in the next operating room, has just had a tumor removed from the bone in his arm. Before the surgery Michael was afraid that he would lose his entire arm. But the surgeon is able to replace the section of cancerous bone with a healthy piece. Although this bone is dead, it will serve as a framework for Michael's own bone to grow into. Eventually, the replacement bone will completely disappear, leaving Michael's own, newly grown, bone in its place.

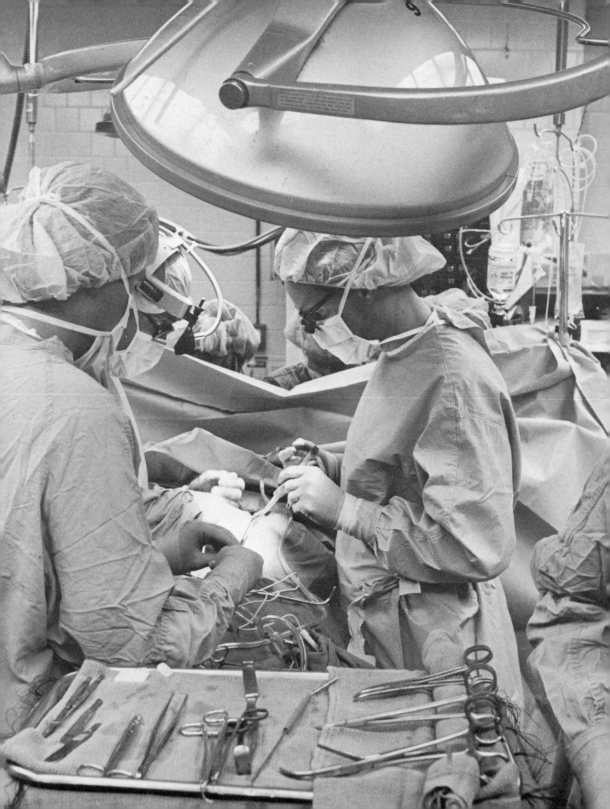

In the third operating room is six-year-old Linda, who awoke one night to find her room in flames. Linda's father saved her life, but he was not able to save her from the serious burns that covered her body. Her skin was so badly burned that Linda had nothing to keep her vital fluids from leaking out of her body, or to prevent deadly bacteria from getting in. The doctors in the operating room are covering her burns with pieces of donated skin to protect her until her own skin has a chance to grow back. Although she will be scarred, Linda will live.

The team of surgeons in the last operating room has already been working for several hours on John, a forty-eight-year-old truck driver who has a bad heart. They are replacing John's diseased heart with one from a younger man who died during the night. Without the new heart, John could not have lived for more than a few more months. Now he could have many healthy years added to his life.

Upstairs in the emergency room, paramedics have just brought sixteen-year-old Randy in by ambulance. Randy had been riding his motorcycle to school when he was struck by a car and seriously injured. The doctor is concerned about the amount of blood Randy has lost and immediately orders a transfusion. After testing a sample of Randy's blood, the nurse hangs a clear plastic bag filled with blood of the right type above the injured boy. A tube carries the lifesaving liquid into the boy's vein.

What do all these patients have in common? Their lives have all either been saved or improved by very special gifts from

In the operating rooms of many hospitals today, doctors and nurses remove organs and tissues from donors, to be given to those whose lives can be saved or greatly improved by the gifts.

people they never knew. The organs and tissues these patients desperately needed were donated to them.

A bank is usually thought of as a place where money can be kept safely until it is needed. But not all banks deal with money. A special group of banks, called **donor banks,** deal with valuable body parts needed to save or improve lives. Donor banks play an important role in medicine today.

Taking organs and tissues from one person and giving them to another is a very complicated process. Although doctors are the ones who usually remove the organs and tissues from the donor, they don't have time to handle the details involved in finding, processing, and transporting the organs and tissues their patients need. These jobs are often handled by the donor banks, also known as organ and tissue banks.

Although they are called banks, organ and tissue banks are different from banks that keep money safe. It is not possible to store most organs the way money and valuables can be stored. Vital organs, such as hearts and livers, must be transplanted within hours of the donor's death. Corneas and kidneys can be kept for only a few days. Blood can be refrigerated for up to forty-two days or frozen for longer periods. Bones and skin can be frozen and stored for years until they are needed.

In many cases, the term *bank*, when it applies to a donor bank, refers to the storage of information rather than the storage of the actual organs. By storing vital information about patients who need transplants, these banks can quickly find recipients for the organs that become available to them.

Most donations of organs and tissues come from people who have just died. Although the donors are dead, their bodies, called **cadavers,** still contain many valuable organs and tissues that can help the living. This is especially true when the donor is killed in an accident rather than dying from a long illness. With the family's permission, certain organs and tissues can be removed from the body and transplanted into patients who need them.

Not all donations are made by people who have died. For

Donor banks often store information rather than actual organs. Like most others, the data base at the United Network for Organ Sharing is computerized.

example, most healthy adults can donate a pint of blood every eight weeks because their bodies quickly replace all the blood that is lost. Sometimes a living donor can save a family member's life by donating a kidney, since most people have two kidneys and can get by quite well with only one. Someone else might donate bone marrow to save the life of a close relative suffering from leukemia, a cancer of the blood.

Organ and tissue banks serve as a source of biological parts to doctors and surgeons who need certain items for their patients. When blood is needed, doctors can get it from a blood bank. Surgeons can get corneas from an eye bank, bones from a bone bank, and skin from a skin bank. An organ bank helps transplant surgeons match patients with hearts, lungs, livers, kidneys, and other vital organs as these items become available.

As tissue and organ transplants become more commonplace and medical research finds new uses for them, the demand on donor banks will become greater. Because of the vital function they serve in today's medicine, donor banks can be referred to as "banks that save lives."

TWO

FROM CELLS
TO SYSTEMS

The human body is a remarkable machine. It begins life as a single, special type of **cell,** a fertilized egg that eventually becomes a full-grown man or woman made up of trillions of cells. Although these cells are so tiny they can only be seen through a microscope, they are complete living organisms. They can take in food and oxygen, release energy, get rid of wastes, and reproduce through division. Each cell contains a full set of "blueprints," or instructions, on how the body is to be built. When the cells divide, each new cell gets a copy of these blueprints.

Cells come in many different sizes and shapes, depending on the work they have to do, but they all share certain similarities. Each cell is enclosed within a protective membrane that is designed to allow food to pass into the cell and waste materials to be expelled. The inside of the cell is filled with a jellylike material called **cytoplasm.** At the center is the **nucleus,** which acts as the cell's control center. The nucleus, with its nucleic acids (such as DNA), determines the specialized work the cell will do. It also controls the cell's growth, repair, and reproduction. When the nucleus dies, so does the cell. Every minute millions of cells in the human body die. However, since healthy cells keep dividing to

AN ANIMAL CELL

The tiny dots on the endoplasmic reticulum are **ribosomes,** which manufacture proteins.

A watery substance called **cytoplasm** fills the cell.

The **cell membrane** controls the entrance and exit of molecules.

The cell **nucleus** controls the activities of the cell and stores genetic information.

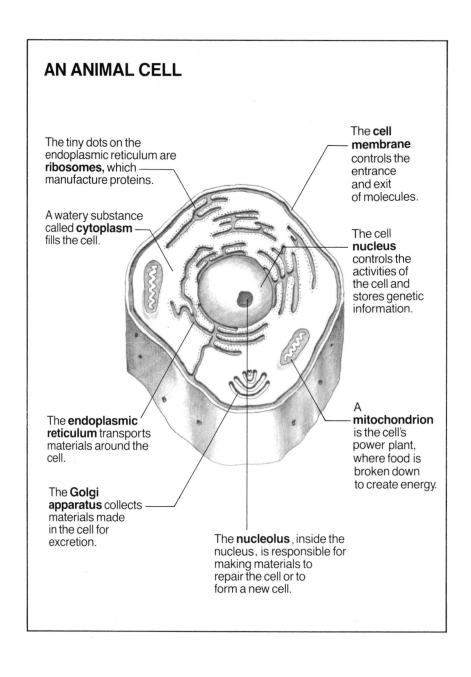

The **endoplasmic reticulum** transports materials around the cell.

The **Golgi apparatus** collects materials made in the cell for excretion.

A **mitochondrion** is the cell's power plant, where food is broken down to create energy.

The **nucleolus**, inside the nucleus, is responsible for making materials to repair the cell or to form a new cell.

A typical cell

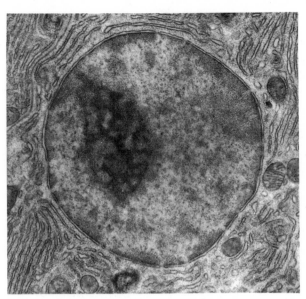

replace them, the number of cells in an adult remains about the same throughout life.

Cells work together in teams, with each team performing a specific job. Those that are alike clump together to form a living sheet of cells, called **tissue.** In this way a group of muscle cells make muscle tissue, nerve cells make nerve tissue, and skin cells make skin tissue.

Different kinds of tissue combine to form **organs** such as the heart, kidneys, or liver. Each organ contains one or more kinds of tissue. For example, the stomach has muscle tissue to churn food and move it to the intestines. Another kind of stomach tissue makes up the soft lining that produces digestive juices. A third kind forms a protective covering for the stomach.

Organs, too, are only part of something bigger. They combine with other organs and tissues to form **systems.** The heart, blood vessels, and blood work together in the circulatory system to

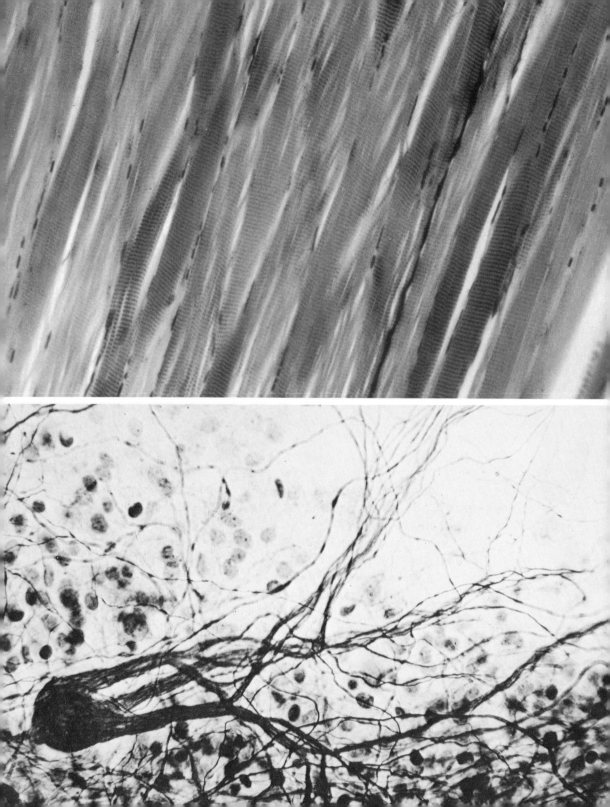

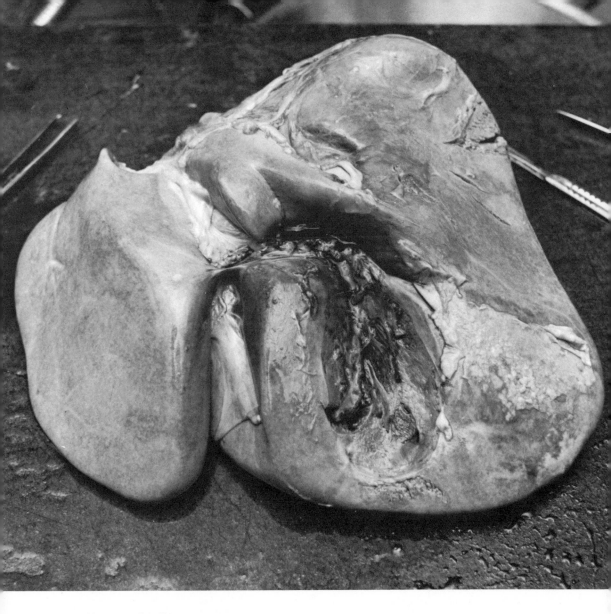

Above: *the liver, an organ that is part of the digestive system.* Opposite above: *muscle.* Opposite below: *nerve tissue*

THE DIGESTIVE SYSTEM

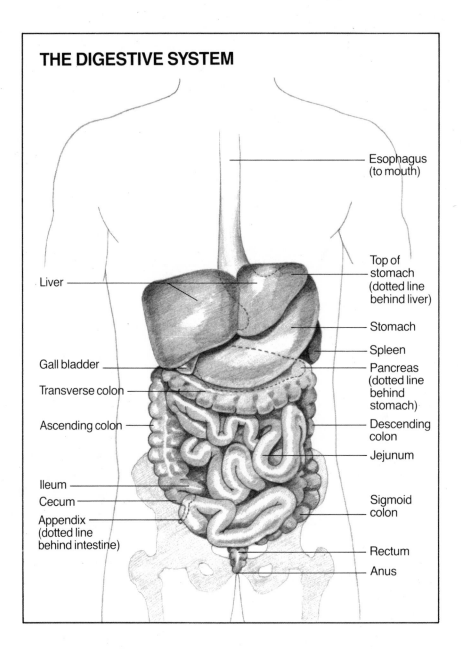

Esophagus
(to mouth)

Top of
stomach
(dotted line
behind liver)

Stomach

Spleen

Pancreas
(dotted line
behind
stomach)

Descending
colon

Jejunum

Sigmoid
colon

Rectum

Anus

Liver

Gall bladder

Transverse colon

Ascending colon

Ileum

Cecum

Appendix
(dotted line
behind intestine)

transport materials around the body. The kidneys and bladder are two important organs in the urinary system, which filters the blood and regulates the amount of water in the body.

All the systems work together as a team to keep the body working properly. The skeletal and muscular systems allow the body to stand and move. The digestive and respiratory systems work to supply the energy the body needs to stay alive and grow. The sensory system collects information that the nervous system either acts upon immediately or stores. The endocrine system distributes hormones to the organs. The reproductive system allows the body to generate new life.

When an organ stops working properly, its entire system may break down. For example, when a heart can no longer pump blood, the circulatory system cannot deliver oxygen and other essential materials to the cells of the body. When the kidneys fail, the urinary system is not able to filter waste products out of the blood, and the patient can become poisoned by the body's own waste. A failed lung keeps the respiratory system from obtaining needed oxygen. When a liver or pancreas fails, the digestive system does not receive all the chemicals it needs to digest food. Also, a diseased liver is unable to remove poisons from the body.

Sometimes artificial methods can be used to replace the function of a failed organ. For example, when the kidneys fail, a **dialysis** machine can take over the job of filtering a patient's blood. But in most cases when a vital organ fails, the patient's only hope is to get a healthy organ to replace it. This is done by means of an organ transplant. If the transplant is successful, the new organ takes over its assigned job in the system, and life goes on.

Although great strides have been made, one serious problem still faces transplant patients. Their bodies often reject the transplanted organs. This rejection is caused by the body's immune system, the same system that works so hard to keep the body well by fighting off diseases and infections. The immune system constantly patrols the body, looking for things that don't belong.

When it discovers foreign bacteria or viruses, it produces disease-fighting proteins, called **antibodies,** to destroy the invaders. Unfortunately, the immune system can't tell the difference between an unfriendly invader, such as a virus, and a friendly invader, such as a transplanted organ. When the immune system discovers the new organ, it produces antibodies to destroy it.

A transplanted organ would not be rejected if the immune system were suppressed, or shut down. However, suppressing the entire system would leave the patient's body defenseless against invading viruses or bacteria. Eventually, the patient would die from disease or infection instead of from the failed organ.

A major breakthrough came in the early 1970s with the discovery of the antirejection drug **cyclosporine.** Instead of suppressing the entire immune system, cyclosporine suppresses only the specific cells within the body that are trying to reject the organ. The drug must be taken every day for life. If the patient stops taking the drug, his or her immune system will recognize the transplanted organ as foreign and will start attacking it.

The more closely a donated organ matches the patient's own body, the milder the rejection will be. When there is enough time, so-called tissue typing can be done to determine how well the donor's organ will match the recipient's tissue type. Tissue types are determined by mixing a person's white cells that contain protein **antigens** with a typing serum. Antigens are substances that stimulate the production of antibodies. Cells that react in the same way form a tissue group or type.

Finding a perfect match between a donor and a recipient is very rare except among identical twins. Tissue typing is done

This immune system cell (the small one), a T-lymphocyte, is attacking two large tumor cells.

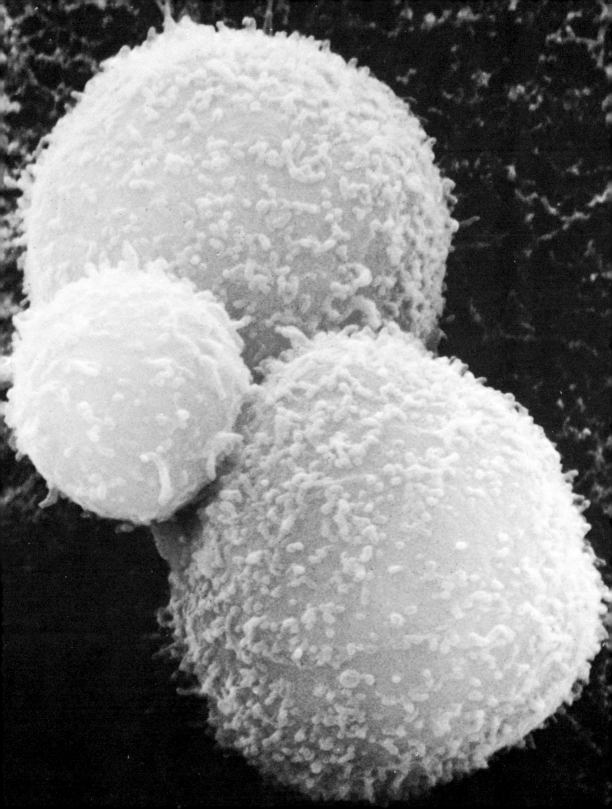

mostly for kidney transplants. There usually isn't time to do it with hearts and livers.

Many people marvel at the ability of surgeons to perform life-saving organ and tissue transplants. But it is even more miraculous that the organs and tissues exist at all. It is doubtful that any person could design such a perfect machine as the human body, with so many different parts, all working together to perform so many important functions. Yet this is exactly what the human body does as it organizes about a hundred trillion cells into the tissues, organs, and systems that keep the body alive and working properly. And this complicated machine got its start as just one tiny cell.

THREE

BLOOD BANKS—
PRESERVING THE FLOW
OF LIFE

No one can live without blood. This precious fluid circulates through the body delivering oxygen and food to every cell. It carries away the waste products these cells produce. To make sure we always have enough, our body makes millions of new blood cells every minute. But sometimes, because of surgery, accidents, or certain diseases, we may need more blood in a hurry. Then we must depend on blood that others have donated to the blood bank.

Almost anyone between the ages of seventeen and sixty-six can donate blood as long as he or she is free of disease and weighs at least 110 pounds (49.5 kg). Unfortunately, only about 5 percent of all eligible donors ever give blood. Some are afraid to donate because they think it will hurt a lot or that they will feel weak afterward. Neither of these things will happen. A few people have the mistaken notion that they can catch diseases, such as AIDS (acquired immune deficiency syndrome), from giving blood. Although it is true that a small percentage of people *receiving* blood contracted AIDS in the past, it is nearly impossible to catch any disease from *donating* blood. New sterilized equipment is used with each donor.

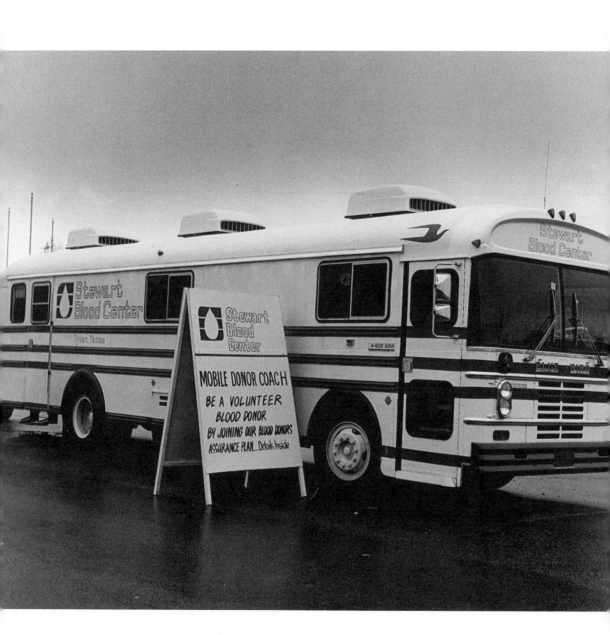

Bloodmobiles are blood banks on wheels.

Most blood is collected during blood drives sponsored by churches, businesses, and other organizations. People find this the most convenient way to donate because it usually doesn't require a trip to a hospital or the blood bank. The bloodmobile, a blood bank on wheels, comes to them.

Jim was in college the first time he donated blood. Until then just the thought of someone taking his blood made him shiver. Jim never considered himself a coward, but he knew he wouldn't be donating blood if he hadn't watched the news that morning. He couldn't forget the image of the tiny girl smiling bravely from her hospital bed. Six-year-old Cindy had leukemia and desperately needed **platelets** that could come only from donations of blood. Jim was touched by Cindy's courage. He wanted to help her even if it meant parting with some of his blood.

Jim was a little nervous when he arrived at the blood bank, but Laura, a nurse's aide, quickly put him at ease. First Laura asked Jim several questions about his health. She wanted to make sure he had never been exposed to diseases that might be passed on through his blood. Next Laura took Jim's temperature and checked his blood pressure and pulse. Finally, she tested a drop of blood from his finger to make sure it contained enough iron.

The health tests took only a few minutes. Like most people, Jim passed them all. Next, Jim relaxed in a special reclining chair. He felt the needle prick the skin on the inside of his arm as a tube was attached to his vein. Jim was surprised to find that, except for the prick when the skin was penetrated, giving blood didn't hurt at all. His blood flowed through a narrow tube into a sterile plastic bag. Inside the bag was a solution to keep the blood from clotting, or forming clumps. There was also a nutrient to keep the **red blood cells** alive. During the donation process the collection bag was kept on a small machine called a shaker that shook the bag just enough to mix the blood with the solution.

It took less than eight minutes for Jim to give a pint of blood, called a unit. Then he joined the other donors at the refreshment

A tiny sample of blood is taken from the donor's finger and tested to make sure the blood contains enough iron.

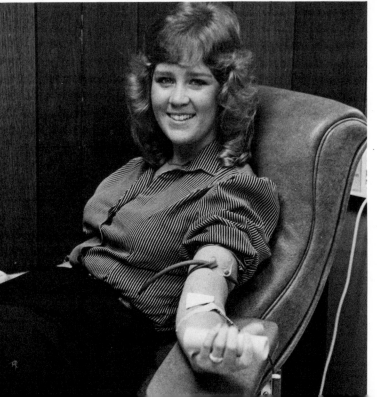

The donor relaxes comfortably for about eight minutes while about a pint of blood is drawn.

area for juice and cookies. The juice helped replace the fluid Jim had lost.

By the time Jim left the blood bank, he felt fine. His body was already rapidly producing new cells to replace the donated blood. In one or two days his plasma would be completely replaced. His red blood cells would be replaced within four to six weeks. In eight weeks Jim's body would be ready to give blood again.

Jim's part of the job was over, but his blood still had many stages to go through before it could help someone. If Jim had watched Laura take the collection bag out of the shaker, he would have noticed that some of his blood had remained in the long tube attached to the bag. Laura had used a special machine to seal off various segments of the tube. This gave the people in the lab plenty of samples of Jim's blood to test without disturbing the blood in the collection bag. An identification number was stamped on the collection bag and on each tiny segment of the tube so there would be no mix-ups.

In the lab, a technician mixed a sample of Jim's blood with certain chemicals to see whether his blood was type A, B, AB, or O. Further testing determined whether his blood was Rh positive or Rh negative. Knowing a donor's blood type—actually, the donor's blood cell type—is extremely important. A patient receiving a transfusion must have blood compatible with his or her own. It is not possible to mix certain blood types. If the wrong type is given, the red blood cells may clump together, clogging the blood vessels. The patient could become very ill or even die. To make sure this doesn't happen, a sample of the donor's blood is carefully crossmatched with a sample of the patient's blood just before a transfusion is given.

Jim's blood was also tested to make sure it didn't contain antibodies for AIDS or hepatitis, two serious diseases that can be passed on through the blood. Blood banks began testing for AIDS in 1985, when it became known that some people had contracted the fatal disease through blood transfusions. New tests now make blood transfusions safer than ever.

A sample from each unit of donated blood must be tested to determine what the blood type is. Sometimes additional tests, such as blood counts, must be made to determine the suitability of donated blood. This picture shows a hematology (blood) lab in a hospital.

After Jim's blood was tested, it was separated into its components, or parts. Normally, patients do not receive transfusions of whole blood. They get a concentrated form of the component they need, such as red blood cells, platelets, **plasma,** or blood products made from plasma. This is not only better for the patient; it also allows one unit of blood to help more than one person.

Soon after Jim's blood was tested, the collection bag containing it was put into a refrigerated **centrifuge,** a machine about the size of a washing machine that spins the blood at a high rate of speed. This spinning causes the blood components to separate. The collection bag has smaller "satellite" bags attached to it with sterile plastic tubes. After the blood was separated, the technician funneled Jim's red blood cells into one of the satellite bags and his platelets into another. The plasma remained in the original bag. Throughout the whole separation process, to keep the blood sterile, it was never exposed to the air.

Each component of blood has its own special job to do. The red blood cells carry oxygen to every part of the body. People with leukemia, anemia, or carbon monoxide poisoning need donations of red blood cells. Red blood cells are also needed by people who have lost a lot of blood. Replacing these cells is the primary reason most patients need transfusions.

Platelets are small fragments of cells that help repair damaged blood vessel walls and aid in blood clotting. They are needed by patients whose bone marrow can no longer produce the platelets they need. Leukemia and some forms of cancer treatment, such as radiation and chemotherapy, can interfere with the body's ability to make platelets.

The white blood cells defend the body against infection. The various kinds of white blood cells are hard to separate from the blood and are not widely used as yet.

More than half of our blood consists of plasma, a straw-colored liquid made up mostly of water. The cells and all other substances of the blood float in the plasma, which also contains

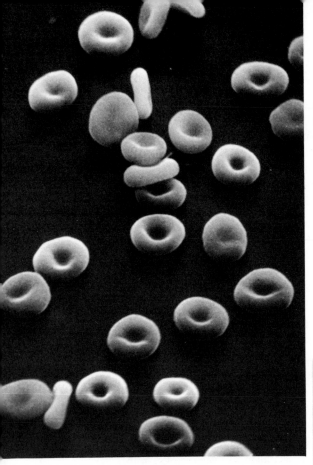

*Normal red
blood cells*

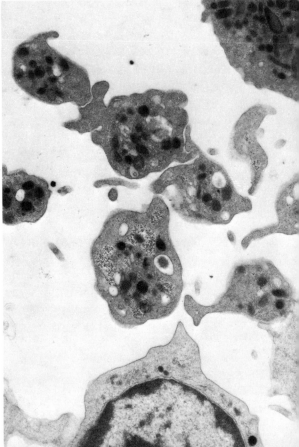

Blood platelets

*A medical centrifuge,
used for separating the
components of blood*

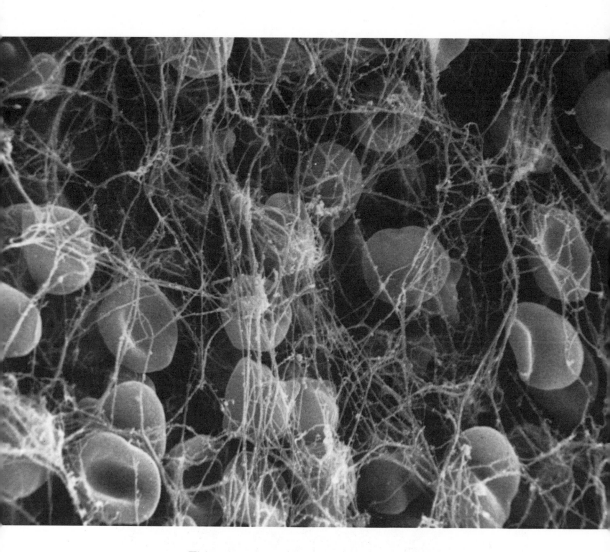

This picture shows a blood clot forming.
The network of fine threads are of the
substance fibrin. Plasma surrounds the clot.
People with hemophilia have blood that
does not clot or clots too slowly.

the coagulation factors of the blood—the ingredients needed to stop bleeding. Plasma is used for patients who develop bleeding during major surgery and for patients in shock. It can also be used in emergency transfusions when the right type of blood isn't available. Since plasma contains no red or white blood cells there is usually no need to match blood types.

Plasma is also used in making several blood products. Some of these products are used by people whose blood is unable to clot because of an inherited blood disease called hemophilia. For them, even a minor injury can cause a great loss of blood. The so-called clotting factor, when removed from plasma, can be given in a concentrated form to people with hemophilia to help stop their bleeding.

Some leukemia and other cancer patients need many transfusions of platelets. Since only a small amount of platelets come from a normal donation, there are often not enough available for these patients. To ease this shortage, some donors give only the platelets from their blood, through a special procedure called **apheresis**. Giving blood in this way is more complicated than a normal donation, but because no red blood cells are given, a person can safely donate platelets twice a week.

An apheresis donor sits in a special chair with tubes placed in the veins of both arms. About a cup of blood is drawn from one arm. It goes into a special machine that spins the blood fast enough to separate it into its components. Specially designed valves make it possible to divert the flow of platelets into a separate pouch. The rest of the blood is warmed and returned to the body through the tube in the other arm. Then more blood is taken out and processed in the same way. The entire procedure takes about an hour and a half. Apheresis donors can watch TV to keep from getting bored while they are donating. This same method can be used when only plasma is needed from the donor.

Blood banks store most of their blood in large refrigerators equipped with alarms to alert technicians if the temperature rises above a certain point. The blood, which is arranged according to

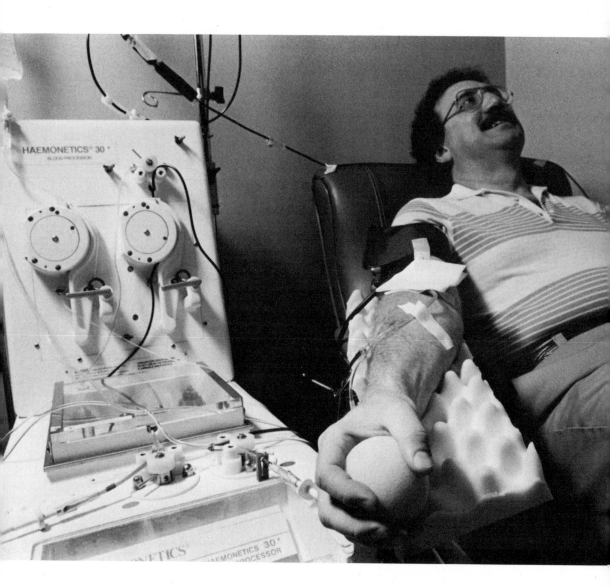

During apheresis, blood taken from one arm is later returned to the body through the other arm, after the plasma or platelets have been removed.

blood type, can be kept from twenty-one to forty-two days, depending on the type of preservative used. Red blood cells can be frozen, but this is an expensive process and is not done by all banks. Plasma can be frozen and kept for a year.

Platelets have the shortest life span. They are kept in packets at room temperature and must be used within seven days. Motorized storage racks constantly turn the packets over. This constant motion keeps the platelets from clumping together. The demand for platelets is so high, there is usually no problem using them up within a few days.

Many people want to be absolutely positive that the blood they receive in surgery will not give them a disease such as AIDS or hepatitis. If they are healthy they can donate their own blood to be saved in the blood bank until they need it.

There is a lot of detail work involved in running a blood bank. Computers are used to keep track of each donation of blood, including where each component went and who received it in a transfusion. Each bank must also keep track of the blood supplies of each hospital it serves. If a certain type of blood is not being used up fast enough at one hospital, it can be transferred to another where it is needed more urgently.

Blood banks do not charge patients for the blood itself, but they do charge a processing fee. This is how the banks get enough money to operate. It is also usually against blood bank policy now to pay donors for their blood. They are afraid this would encourage some donors to not be completely truthful in answering the health questions, which could affect the quality of the blood. There are, however, some places where donors are paid. Some commercial companies who make and sell blood products pay donors for plasma collected through apheresis. This blood is not used for transfusions.

Approximately four million patients a year receive blood transfusions. Blood banks must work continually to keep up with this constant need. Sometimes the banks run dangerously low in their supply of blood. Their job would be much easier if more people would become blood donors. As it is now, the lives of many people depend on the generosity of relatively few. As long as there are enough donors, blood banks will give us the security of knowing that if we ever need blood in a hurry, a safe supply will be there waiting for us.

FOUR

EYE BANKS—
TURNING DARKNESS
INTO LIGHT

The harsh ring of the telephone awoke Jan. As she fumbled in the darkness to answer, she glanced at the clock next to her bed. It was 4:30 in the morning. As a technician for the eye bank, Jan was used to having her sleep interrupted. The message from the hospital was brief. A twenty-year-old man had died an hour earlier in an automobile accident. His family had agreed to donate the corneas from his eyes.

Jan was completely awake by the time she hung up. She dressed quickly, grabbed her equipment, and hurried to the hospital. She knew there was no time to waste. The cornea, which is the clear covering that protects the front of each eye like a watch crystal, has to be removed within six hours of the donor's death. After that, it begins to deteriorate and cannot be used to restore someone's sight.

As soon as Jan reached the hospital, she met with the young man's parents to offer her sympathy and to thank them for their donation. Sharing in the family's grief is the most difficult part of Jan's job, but one she considers very important. When all their questions had been answered, the donor's parents signed the consent form giving Jan permission to remove their son's corneas.

CROSS SECTION OF THE HUMAN EYE

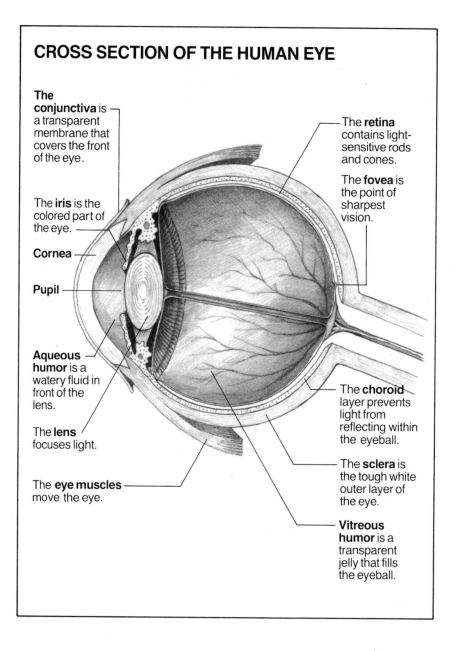

The conjunctiva is a transparent membrane that covers the front of the eye.

The **iris** is the colored part of the eye.

Cornea

Pupil

Aqueous humor is a watery fluid in front of the lens.

The **lens** focuses light.

The **eye muscles** move the eye.

The **retina** contains light-sensitive rods and cones.

The **fovea** is the point of sharpest vision.

The **choroid** layer prevents light from reflecting within the eyeball.

The **sclera** is the tough white outer layer of the eye.

Vitreous humor is a transparent jelly that fills the eyeball.

Next, Jan checked the young man's medical records to make sure there were no conditions present that might disqualify him as a donor. She then went to the hospital's morgue where the body had been taken. With the skill that comes from many years of practice, Jan carefully removed the corneas from the donor's eyes. She put each one in a small bottle containing a chemical preservative.

Sometimes Jan removes whole eyes, replacing them with plastic eye caps. With their eyes closed, these donors still look normal for their funeral. Today, Jan took only the corneas. Since they are clear, their removal did not noticeably change the donor's appearance.

Jan took the precious corneas back to her office at the eye bank. She examined them under her **slit-lamp,** an instrument used to examine eyes and named for the high-intensity beam of light that is projected through a narrow slit. The combination of intense light and powerful magnifying lens gave Jan a clear view of the corneas. They were in excellent condition. There were no signs of cloudiness, damage, or disease. Jan put the corneas back into their bottles of preservative, then into the eye bank's refrigerator. With newer preservatives the corneas can now be kept for up to fourteen days, but most surgeons still prefer to transplant them within three days.

Next, Jan turned her attention to the list of people waiting for corneas. It always bothered her that this list was so long and that the names moved to the top so slowly. The two names at the top had been waiting for several months. Jan called their surgeons to give them the good news.

Across town, Mary, a young mother of three, was fixing breakfast for her family. The telephone startled her. For a moment Mary couldn't make herself answer it. She knew she was at the top of the list to receive a cornea. She had spent nearly a week both hoping for, and dreading, the call that would send her to the hospital. Mary had put off having the surgery for many years. She knew a corneal transplant could help her, but the

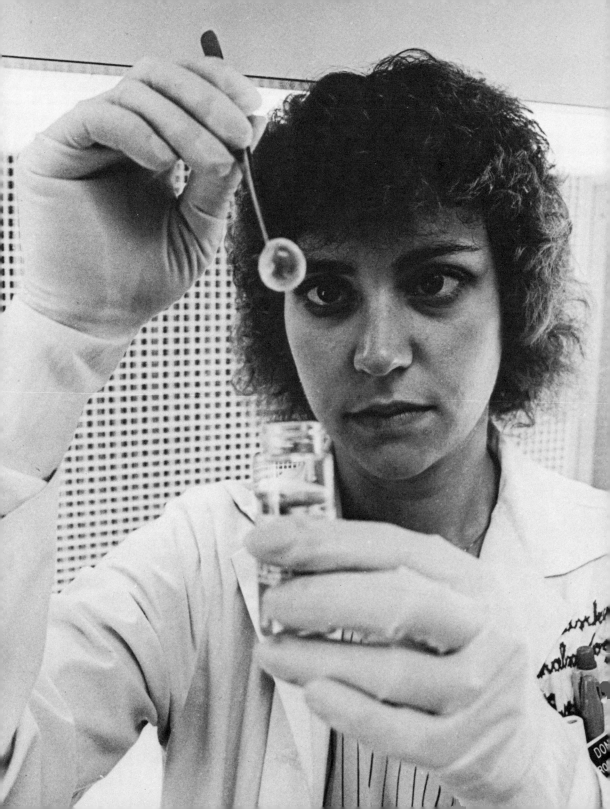

thought of someone operating on her eyes frightened her. Finally, her desire for a normal life became so great that she agreed to have the surgery.

For Mary, the nightmare that had begun five years earlier was coming to an end. She still remembered the horrible day when her eye doctor first told her she was losing her sight. An inherited eye disease was causing her corneas to become cone-shaped. Light hitting her eyes became distorted. The problem slowly grew worse until Mary could no longer see clearly. She had to give up her driver's license. She couldn't tell if the cookies she was baking were too brown, or if the shirts she ironed were free of wrinkles. She even had to take her children to a neighbor when they were hurt because she couldn't see how serious their injuries were.

In the operating room the next morning, Mary's eye surgeon used an instrument called a **trephine** to remove a thin circle of damaged cornea from Mary's eye. The trephine, which works like a tiny cookie cutter, was then used to remove an identical circle from the donated cornea. Like fitting a piece into a jigsaw puzzle, the surgeon placed the new cornea into Mary's eye. He stitched it into place with thread finer than a human hair. When he was finished, he tightly bandaged Mary's eye.

The next morning Mary's bandages were removed. When the layers of gauze had been peeled off, Mary blinked a few times, then peered out through half-closed eyes. She was surprised to find that she could see better already, although her vision was

The procurement director for an eye bank examines a donated cornea to make sure it is suitable for transplantation.

—43—

still far from normal. Medication used to help the healing would continue to blur her vision for a while. But even on this first day Mary had seen enough to know that life was going to be much better. Now that she knew how easy the surgery was, she looked forward to having her other cornea replaced in several months.

Corneal transplants are only done on one eye at a time. This allows two people to enjoy improved vision instead of just one. It is also done as a safety precaution. In case of infection or rejection, only one eye would be affected instead of both.

A corneal transplant is successful 95 percent of the time. The age of the patient doesn't seem to matter. Successful transplants have been done on a 9-day-old baby as well as a 103-year-old great-grandfather. There is usually no problem with rejection because there are no blood vessels in the cornea. The only matching that is done is by age. Surgeons wouldn't give a tiny baby the corneas from a forty-year-old-man.

There are many situations in which a person might need a corneal transplant. The disease Mary had, called keratoconus, is quite common. Other people need transplants when their corneas cloud over after being injured, such as from glass fragments or acid getting in their eyes. The eyes of still others become cloudy or swollen from infections or other diseases. Every once in a while a baby is born with cloudy corneas that can be replaced when the baby is only a few months old.

Only the best corneas are used for transplants, but no eyes are wasted. Those not suitable for restoring sight are used in

Sports figures such as Artis Gilmore of the San Antonio Spurs help make people more aware of the great need for donated eyes.

NAME OR ADDRESS CHANGE REQUIRES DUPLICATE LICENSE WITHIN 30 DAYS
RESTRICTION CODE
A WITH CORRECTIVE LENSES
B LOFS AGE 18 OR OLDER
C DAYTIME ONLY
D NOT TO EXCEED 45 MPH
E NO EXPRESSWAY DRIVING
I M/C NOT TO EXCEED 125 CC
J LICENSED M/C OPERATOR 18 OR OVER IN SIGHT
K MOPED
P STATED ON LICENSE
Q LOFS 18 OR OVER VEHICLE ABOVE CLASS B
R LOFS 18 OR OVER VEHICLE ABOVE CLASS C
S OUTSIDE MIRROR OR HEARING AID
T AUTOMATIC TRANSMISSION
U APPLICABLE PROSTHETIC DEVICE
V APPLICABLE VEHICLE DEVICES
W POWER STEERING
ALLERGIC REACTION TO DRUGS
DONOR'S CERTIFICATION – I, THE UNDERSIGNED, BEING OF SOUND MIND AND OVER AGE 18, DONATE MY Eyes AS AN ANATOMICAL GIFT AT THE TIME OF MY DEATH, UNDER PROVISIONS OF ART. 6687bVCS AND IN CONFORMITY WITH ART. 4590-2 VCS.
WITNESS
SIGNATURE
WITNESS

valuable research projects. By studying abnormalities in eyes, researchers can learn more about the causes and treatments of blindness and other eye problems. In 1985, U.S. eye banks provided 25,000 eyes to help researchers in their fight against blindness.

Donated corneas have recently been used to improve the vision of people who cannot be helped with regular contact lenses or glasses. The corneas are frozen, then ground and shaped into a lens to fit a particular patient. This new lens is attached to the patient's cornea and helps the eye to focus. Cells from the patient's cornea eventually grow into the new lens, turning it into a living contact lens. This operation is helpful to people, especially children, who have had cataract surgery and cannot manage contacts. It can also help those who are extremely farsighted or nearsighted.

Eye banks have helped thousands of people overcome blindness. The Eye Bank Association of America estimates that 25,000 Americans received corneal transplants in 1985. Unfortunately, that left up to 5,000 people still on waiting lists. There are never enough corneas available to take care of everyone who needs one. Some states are trying to do something about this shortage by passing a law of "presumed consent." This allows eyes to be removed from anyone sent to the medical examiner unless someone from the family objects. Medical examiners most often do autopsies on victims of homicide, suicide, and death from unknown causes.

Corneal transplants cannot help all people with vision problems, only those whose sight is blocked by defective corneas. There are many other causes of blindness that cannot be helped. Still, millions of people throughout the world are enjoying the gift of restored sight. Without eye banks and the generosity of donors and their families, these people would still be living their lives in darkness.

FIVE

ORGAN BANKS—
REPLACING DAMAGED HEARTS,
LIVERS, AND KIDNEYS

Eleven-year-old Kelly bounced on the back of her friend's three-wheeled motorcycle as they rumbled along the shoulder of a rural Michigan road. There was no traffic, nothing to spoil their fun—until they hit a deep rut in their path. The jolt tossed Kelly into the air. Her head slammed against the hard pavement.

Kelly was alive but unconscious when the ambulance brought her to the hospital. Throughout the long night her parents watched and prayed for some sign of recovery, but Kelly didn't improve. By dawn her injured brain could no longer control her breathing, so Kelly was put on a machine called a **respirator** that kept her body breathing artificially.

The next day the doctor ran special tests on Kelly. He shined a light into her eyes, but the pupils did not contract to block out the light. He tested her for pain, but she made no response. He ran other tests, but nothing happened. Finally, the doctor took Kelly off the respirator for three minutes. She did not start breathing on her own. Although her heart continued to beat, her other functions were being performed mechanically by the respirator. The doctor sadly told Kelly's parents that their child was **brain dead.**

During Kelly's struggle for life, her parents decided that if she died they would donate her organs. They felt it was what Kelly would have wanted. Soon after the doctor signed the death certificate, Kelly's parents signed the consent form, giving permission for her organs to be removed. The hospital notified the local organ bank immediately to let them know that an organ donor was available. This set into motion the complicated process of retrieving and transplanting Kelly's organs.

When the call came into the organ bank in mid-afternoon, it was answered by Marge. As an experienced procurement coordinator, Marge was responsible for organizing the many details involved in procuring, or getting, the organs and transporting them to the proper transplant hospitals. Her job was a race against time. Vital organs, such as hearts, livers, and kidneys, cannot be stored. They must be removed from the body of the donor and transplanted into the recipients as soon as possible.

Marge hurried to the hospital, where she studied Kelly's medical records. There were no signs of any serious diseases that would keep her from being a good donor. All the required tests had been run. Marge was satisfied that Kelly's body was being maintained correctly to keep her organs in good condition. If Kelly's parents had not already signed the consent form, Marge would have talked to them, asking for their permission. That was not necessary today.

Next, Marge went to look at Kelly. The sight of a donor, especially such a young one, never failed to produce a lump in Marge's throat. Kelly was dead, but her heart was still beating and she was still breathing. The respirator was keeping her organs alive and supplied with oxygen until arrangements could be made for their removal. But keeping her on the respirator too long could reduce the quality of the organs.

Back at her office, Marge telephoned several transplant centers to see if they had need of Kelly's organs. Besides telephones, most organ banks use computers to help them place organs. By typing a donor's weight, blood type, age, and sex into a computer they can find the most suitable recipients. Most organ banks belong to networks such as the Organ Procurement and Transplantation Network. This and many smaller networks serve as clearinghouses to match available organs with patients waiting for transplants.

In determining who shall receive organs, those on the waiting list with the most urgent need are considered first. Then come those high on the waiting list whose needs are less urgent. For all organs, the donor and recipient must have the same blood type. For hearts and livers, the donor and recipient should be roughly the same size and weight. Kidneys must be matched more carefully, so tests are run to determine the tissue types of the donor and recipient.

Distance must also be considered in choosing organ recipients. People who live too far away are turned down when there isn't enough time to remove the organ, transport it, and transplant it. Most organ banks prefer to distribute the organs in their own area unless there is an urgent need somewhere else.

In working with the transplant centers to place Kelly's organs, Marge dealt mainly with facts and figures. But behind those cold facts were four very real people whose lives were about to be dramatically changed.

Eleven-year-old Felicia lay in the intensive-care unit of a hospital in Virginia. She had been born with a hole in her heart that had damaged one of the organ's valves. In spite of several operations, Felicia's heart had grown worse and was now barely keeping her alive. It was not expected to last much longer. Only a new heart could save her.

At her home in South Carolina, ten-year-old Sherri was trying to stay alive in spite of a severely scarred liver caused by an enzyme deficiency. The damaged liver began to divert blood into Sherri's stomach. She had almost bled to death three times in the past five months. Without a new liver, Sherri would die. To be

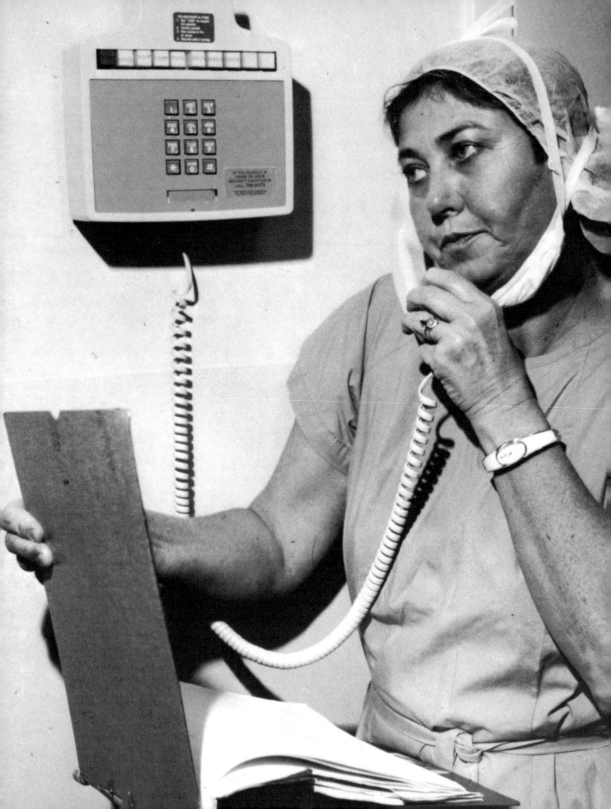

Opposite: *the telephone is an important tool for an organ procurement coordinator as she assists in matching patients with available organs and handles the many details of the procurement-transplant procedure.*
Above: *most organ banks belong to networks and serve as clearinghouses to match available organs with patients waiting for transplants.*

sure no time was wasted in getting her to the hospital in Pittsburgh if a liver became available, Sherri's father wore a special paging device on his belt at all times.

Although he was not close to death, thirty-one-year-old Brad was not able to lead a normal life. Brad's kidneys no longer worked to filter the impurities from his blood. For four hours a session, three days a week, Brad had to have dialysis, which meant being attached to a dialysis machine that cleansed his blood for him. He hated scheduling his life around the machine and hated the way it made him feel. A new kidney was the only thing that could give him a normal life. Brad's name had been on a waiting list for more than a year. The wait had become unbearable.

Fifty miles (80 km) away, thirty-three-year-old Al was in serious condition with a failed kidney. Al had faithfully attached himself to his home dialysis machine three times a week for two years. Although many people do very well on a dialysis machine, Al did not. His condition grew worse until he was too weak to work or to do most of the things he used to enjoy. His doctors became alarmed at Al's rapidly failing condition. He was given priority status on the list of those waiting for kidneys.

As these four approached the end of their long wait, Marge continued making the necessary arrangements for removing and transporting Kelly's organs. Teams of doctors had to be notified, an operating room for Kelly had to be scheduled, and arrangements had to be made for the doctors who would operate on Kelly to be picked up at the airport. Marge was constantly on the telephone, checking with the procurement coordinators at the three transplant centers who were scrambling to make sure everything was ready on their end. They were busy making the travel arrangements for their "recovery" or "retrieval" teams, as well as notifying the recipients and scheduling operating rooms for them. Everything had to work like clockwork.

That night the transplant teams flew to Kelly's hospital from three states. Sometimes the donor is flown to the recipient's hos-

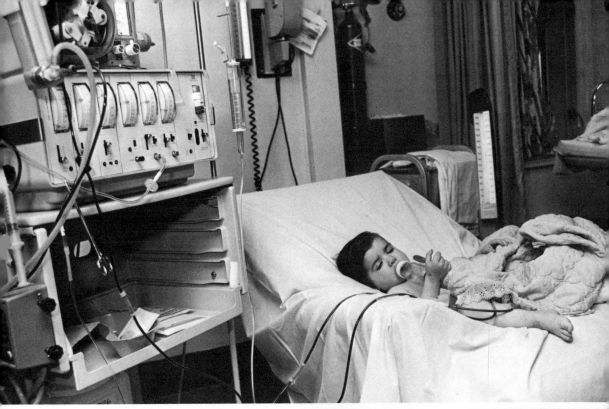

A young child on a
dialysis machine.
The filtering com-
ponent of the ma-
chine can be seen
in the picture below.

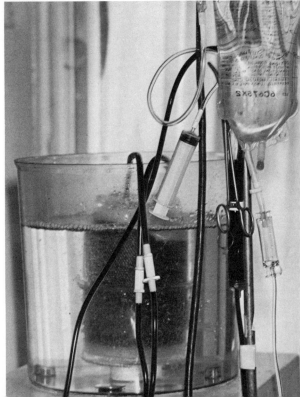

pital. This method cuts down on the amount of time an organ is out of the body, but it has drawbacks. Air travel can sometimes upset the physical condition of the donor. It also puts more stress on the donor's family, who may not be willing to have their loved one shipped across the country.

It was two o'clock the following morning when the transplant teams gathered at the hospital. Kelly's body, still connected to the respirator, was wheeled into the operating room. When everyone was ready, the machine was turned off. The beeping and hissing stopped, but the surgeons were so intent on the task that lay ahead that they hardly noticed. Their job now was to save lives, and they had to work against the clock to do it.

Organs are removed in a certain order. When the heart is being donated, the heart team goes first because they have the shortest time in which to complete their task. In Kelly's case, they had less than six hours to remove the heart, fly it back to Virginia, and have it beating in Felicia's chest. It took less than ten minutes for them to remove the heart. They placed it in an icy slush, packed it in a plastic container, then put it into a small picnic cooler filled with ice. Without wasting a minute, they rushed from the hospital to the ambulance, which would whisk them to the airport. Their waiting jet had priority clearance and took off within minutes of their arrival. As they left, Marge called their hospital and told them when to expect the heart.

Felicia was already in the operating room in Virginia. Her heart was ready to be removed the instant Kelly's heart arrived there.

The liver was the next organ to be removed. Although the surgeons had twelve hours to work with, their job was much more complicated than the heart team's job had been. It took nearly four hours for them to complete the difficult task of remov-

A human heart

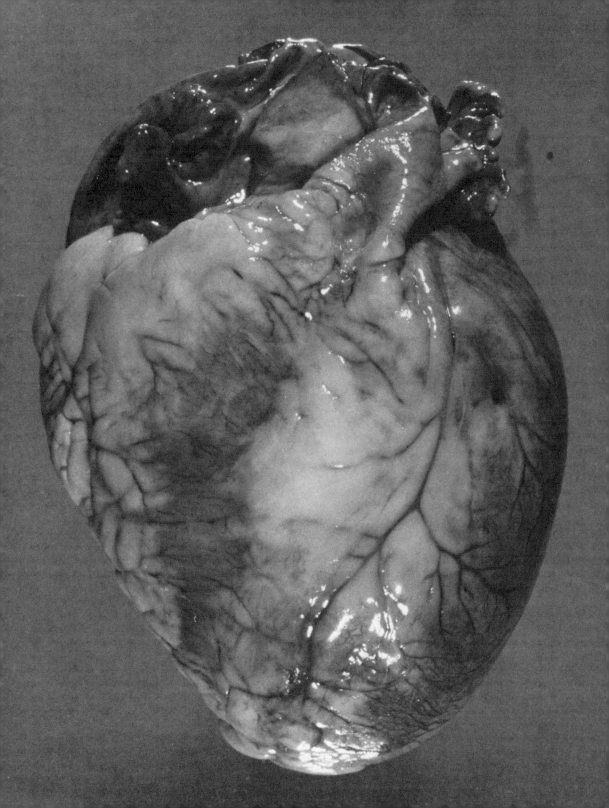

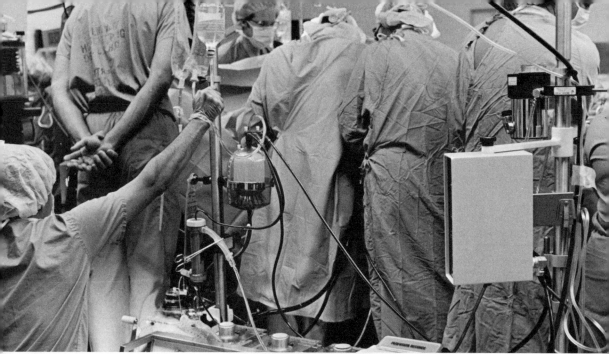

Above: *while the heart transplant team works against the clock to exchange hearts, the patient is kept alive on a heart-lung machine.*
Right: *a heart transplant surgeon holds the gift of life in his hands.*

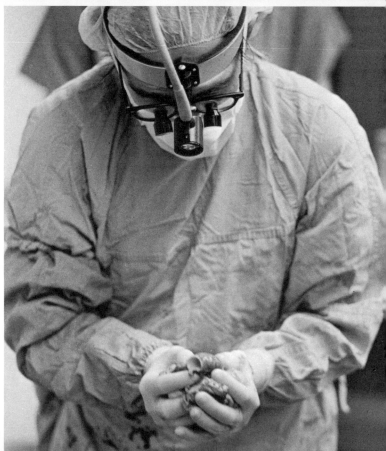

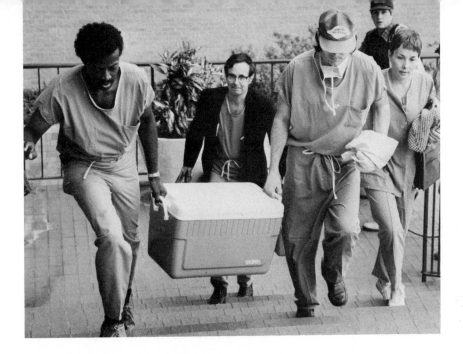

An organ-harvesting team rushes back to their hospital with a donated heart packed safely in ice in a picnic cooler.

ing Kelly's liver. They packed it in ice in plastic containers, just as the heart had been packed. The surgeons rushed back to the jet with their precious cargo. Marge called the hospital in Pittsburgh to let them know when the liver would arrive. Sherri's surgery had already begun. By the time her new liver arrived safely, her damaged organ would already have been removed. It would take the surgeons many more hours of complicated surgery to connect Sherri's new liver to the many tiny blood vessels, veins, and arteries.

Once the liver was out, the kidney team got their turn. The kidneys were removed and packed in an icy slush, just as the heart and liver had been. Kidneys packed this way can be kept for up to forty-eight hours. Quite often kidneys are not packed in ice. They are put on a **perfusion pump,** which circulates the chilled liquid. With this method they can be kept for up to seventy-two hours.

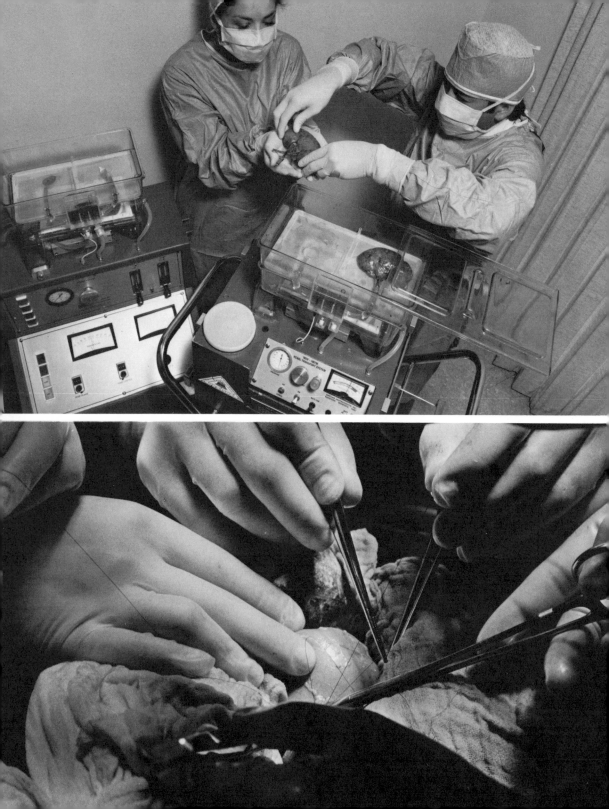

Because kidneys don't have to be transplanted immediately, they can be flown on commercial airlines when necessary. Styrofoam coolers containing the ice-packed kidneys are placed in a box with "Human Kidneys" printed on the side. The box is kept in the galley of the plane or some other safe place in the cabin. If the kidneys are to be kept on a perfusion pump, two first-class tickets must be purchased—one for the coordinator and one for the pump.

Some transplant teams prefer to reverse the order in which the donor's organs are removed. They leave the respirator on while they remove the liver, kidneys, and any other needed organs. The heart is removed last, just after the respirator is turned off. This method shortens the amount of time the organs must go without blood.

The donation of Kelly's organs changed the lives of four people. Instead of lying in a hospital bed like a rag doll, Felicia now spends her days running, swimming, and riding her skateboard. Al and Brad are delighted with the changes the new kidneys have made in their lives. They both have more energy than they have had in years. One of the best days of Al's life was the day the dialysis machine was wheeled out of his house.

Sherri's body at first rejected her new liver, but with drugs the doctors were able to dramatically improve her condition. Almost all transplanted organs show some degree of rejection. Doctors must know the extent of their patient's rejection so they can adjust the amount of medication given. The most effective means

Above: *donated kidneys can be placed on a perfusion pump, which circulates an icy slush through the organs.* Below: *the final suturing (stitching) of a donor's kidney to a recipient's arteries*

of determining rejection is through a **biopsy**. A tiny bit of tissue is removed from the organ using a tube with little "pinchers" at the end. The tissue is examined under a microscope. If rejection is present, the tissue will have an excessive number of white blood cells. Biopsies are taken soon after transplant surgery and routinely after the patients have recovered. Transplant patients must take antirejection drugs, such as cyclosporine, for the rest of their lives, but it is a small price to pay for living.

Of all donor banks, organ banks face the most critical shortages. One problem is that only people who die in certain ways can donate vital organs such as hearts, livers, lungs, and kidneys. They must die from an injury that will not affect their transplantable organs. Most donors declared as brain dead have died from accidents, gunshot wounds to the head, or strokes. It is also necessary that organ donors die in the hospital while they are on life-support machines. If someone dies even minutes before they can reach the hospital, their organs cannot be used. They can, however, donate other tissues, such as corneas, bones, and skin.

The brain-death requirement eliminates many potential organ donors. But even among those who are eligible, only about one-sixth actually become donors. Since most people do not make their wishes known before their death, the decision to donate organs must be made by the donor's next of kin. Most families do not think of organ donation in the midst of their grief, or perhaps do not know enough about it to make the decision. In most cases, they are never even asked to donate.

Organ banks are attempting to solve these problems. Through advertising campaigns, articles in magazines and newspapers, and speeches to schools and organizations, they try to make the public more aware of the need for organ donations. They hope that greater public awareness will encourage families to discuss their feelings about organ donation long before a death actually occurs. Organ banks also conduct training sessions for doctors and nurses to make them more aware of potential organ donors and let them know who to contact when a donor becomes available. Some states are even passing laws requiring hospitals to discuss organ donation with all potential donors or their families.

Through education and legislation, perhaps someday there will be enough organs for all who need them. Organ banks are working toward this goal. A large blue button worn by an organ bank worker sums up the way most people there feel. It says, "Don't take your organs to heaven. Heaven knows we need them here."

SIX

BONE BANKS— REBUILDING THE BODY'S FRAMEWORK

Michael loved team sports. Football, basketball, baseball, soccer—he played them all. In spite of a sore arm, Michael served as quarterback for his sophomore football team and contributed to their winning season. He wasn't too concerned about the pain in his arm until baseball season, when it interfered with his pitching. A routine X-ray revealed that his problem was more serious than anyone expected. Michael had a malignant bone tumor.

Many years ago the diagnosis of a bone tumor would have been devastating news. Michael's arm might have required amputation. Perhaps surgeons would have tried holding the bones together with a metal rod, but normally this doesn't work well with active young people. Michael's story had a happy ending, however. The surgeon removed a 4-inch (10-cm) segment of tumorous bone from Michael's arm and replaced it with a segment of cadaver bone from the bone bank.

Inside Michael's arm the piece of donor bone slowly did a disappearing act. Although the bone was dead, it served as a framework for new bone to grow into. Eventually, the transplanted bone completely disappeared, leaving Michael's newly formed bone in its place.

The complete replacement of bone happens only with bone that is porous. If whole bones or large sections of compact bone are transplanted, the ends will fuse with the patient's bone, but the entire bone will not be replaced. In this case the transplanted bone serves to fill in the empty space left by the removal of the diseased bone. It will never be quite as strong as the original bone, but it can save a limb from amputation.

Some surgeons prefer to use bone taken from the patient's own body when they need to do a bone graft. Although this bone may adapt to the patient's body more quickly and presents no problems of rejection, it requires surgery on two areas instead of one. This means longer surgery, more blood loss, and a longer, more painful recovery. Today, more surgeons are turning to bone banks to get the bone their patients need.

With a few exceptions, banks get their bones from donors who have just died. Although it is best to take the bones as soon after death as possible, timing is not as critical as it is with vital organs. Bones can be removed within twelve hours of the donor's death, or within twenty-four hours if the cadaver has been kept in cold storage. As with other organ and tissue donations, the family's permission is needed before bone can be removed. Also, the donor's medical records and blood tests must be examined to make sure the donor is free from diseases or infections that would affect the quality of the bone.

Different banks handle the removal of bones in different ways. Most banks prefer to remove the bones in an operating room, under sterile conditions. However, it is also possible to remove them in a clean, but not necessarily sterile, environment as long as the bones are properly sterilized later. These bones can be exposed to gases, such as ethylene oxide, to eliminate infectious organisms. No matter which method is used, many tests are done during the various stages of removal and processing to ensure that the bone is sterile.

An average of eleven to twenty bones are taken from each cadaver, depending on the wishes of the donor's family. These

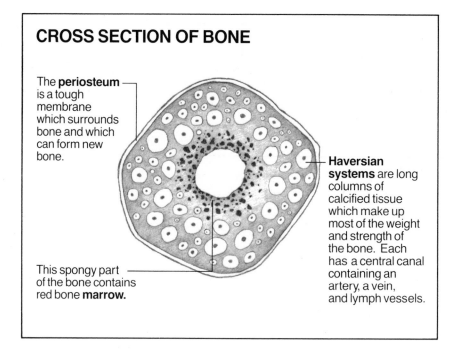

CROSS SECTION OF BONE

The **periosteum** is a tough membrane which surrounds bone and which can form new bone.

Haversian systems are long columns of calcified tissue which make up most of the weight and strength of the bone. Each has a central canal containing an artery, a vein, and lymph vessels.

This spongy part of the bone contains red bone **marrow.**

include the long bones of the legs, illium (hip bone), ribs, elbow and shoulder joints, and sometimes the jaw bones. Usually the bones in the hands and face are not removed unless the donor is to be cremated. When all the bones have been removed, the donor's skeleton is reconstructed using round wooden rods and plaster. This ensures that the donor will look presentable at the funeral.

Unless the bones are going to be used right away, they must be preserved. Whole bones and large sections are usually frozen at very low temperatures. First, all the soft tissue and bone marrow must be removed, either by cutting it off or washing it off with a high-pressure water hose. Then the bones are cut into various shapes and sizes and put into a special slow-cooling liquid nitrogen freezer. Once the bones have reached −70 degrees Celsius or lower, they can be transferred to larger liquid nitrogen freezers, where they can be kept for years. Smaller bone banks can freeze the bone in a regular deep freeze as long as special precautions are taken. As a safety feature, all freezers have alarms that sound if the temperature rises above a certain point.

Bones are kept frozen until they are taken into the operating room to be used. They can be thawed quickly in a warm saltwater solution, then cut and shaped into the size needed.

Most smaller bones are preserved by freeze-drying. As with the other bones, all the soft tissue must be removed; the bones are then cut into various shapes. Some are cut into tiny, porous cubes resembling salad croutons. Others are cut into blocks, chips, or match-stick shapes. Still other bones are ground into a powder. Bones such as jaw bones and ribs are often left whole.

After the bones have been prepared, they are put into the freeze-drier. Here they are exposed to gas to sterilize them, then slowly frozen. While the freeze-drier lowers the temperature to between −60 and −70 degrees Celsius, a vacuum slowly sucks the water out of the bone. Freeze-dried bones are stored in airtight bottles or packages. Just like freeze-dried coffee, they can be kept on a shelf at room temperature for years.

There are many uses for donor bone. Large pieces can be used to replace bone that has been removed because of tumors or other defects. Small wedges cut from the hip bone can be used to help those with spinal problems. Healthy joints can replace those that no longer work because of injuries or arthritis. Slivers of bone can straighten crooked spines, and bone powder can stimulate bone growth in jaws that no longer have a firm hold on teeth. A paste made by mixing bone powder with a saline solution can fill in small holes and cracks in bone and promote new bone growth. A few specialized bone banks even save the tiny bones of the ear, which, in rare cases, can be transplanted to restore hearing.

Above: *bones can be cut into various shapes and sizes before drying.* Right: *jars containing pieces of bone are placed in a freeze-drier, which sucks ice crystals out of the bones during the freezing process.*

Bottles and packets of dried bones can be kept for years on the storeroom shelf.

Not all bone banks are looking for perfect bone specimens to transplant. Sixty-year-old Harry has been deaf since he was a child. His friend Franklin has had trouble with his balance for nearly ten years. Both of these men are perfect donors for the National Temporal Bone Banks Program. These banks need donors of any age who have hearing or balance problems to donate their temporal bones for research.

The temporal bones are very hard bones found inside the skull. Protected inside these bones are the eardrum, the external ear canal, the middle and inner ear, and the nerve tissues that connect to the brain. Since the tiny bones and membranes of the ear are surrounded by the temporal bones, they cannot safely be

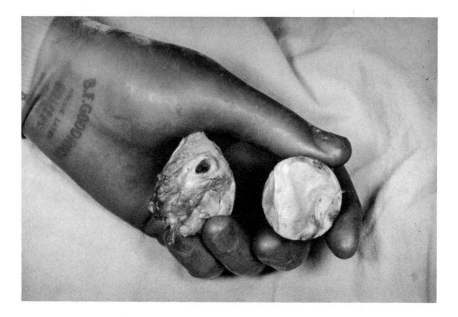

Temporal bones, which form the structure of the middle and inner ear, are used for research into the causes and treatment of ear diseases.

studied during a person's lifetime. But after death, the temporal bones of the donor can easily and quickly be removed during a regular autopsy. This can be done at a hospital or even a funeral home. The operation does not deform the donor's face, head, or neck. Once removed, the temporal bones can be used for research into the causes of deafness, as well as other hearing and balance problems. Some of the bones are used by medical schools to train young physicians in ear care. With these bones they learn about the structure of the ear and improve their surgical skills.

Most bone banks share a similar problem—shortages. There is never enough bone to meet the increasing demands. One reason is that most potential donors have never heard of bone banks and don't realize their bones can be used. Also, there isn't as much glamor in donating bones as there is in donating a heart or kidney that might save someone's life.

Through bone banks, pieces of bone from those who no longer can use them are easing pain, saving limbs, helping young bodies grow up straight, and filling in spaces left by accidents or cancer. Although bone banks usually don't help save lives, they can reduce pain and improve the quality of life for many people.

SEVEN

SKIN BANKS—
SUPPLYING LIVING
BANDAGES

While twenty-eight-year-old William was working on a house in Las Vegas, the floor sealant he was using ignited. Caught in a flash of flames, William barely escaped with his life. He was rushed to the hospital with severe burns over 90 percent of his body.

In treating serious burns such as William's, it is important to cover the burned areas with new skin as quickly as possible. The skin keeps in body fluids and keeps out deadly bacteria that cause infections. It also reduces the amount of pain the patient experiences. Whenever possible, pieces of skin are taken from the unburned parts of a patient's body and a **skin graft** is done over the burned areas. But in very extensive burns, such as William's, the patient doesn't have undamaged skin to spare. A substitute must be found. Although antibiotic creams, pigskin, and artificial skin are sometimes used, most burn specialists agree that skin from a skin bank is the next best thing to a patient's own skin.

Skin banks get their skin from cadavers. The donors do not have to be brain dead and kept on life-support machines. They just need to have been healthy, with no history of diseases such as cancer, hepatitis, AIDS, or infections that could be passed along to the recipient. The best donors are between the ages of fourteen and seventy. Small children don't have enough skin to donate.

When a skin bank is notified that there is a donor, a technician or procurement coordinator is sent out to remove the skin. Timing is not quite as critical as it is with other organs. The skin can be recovered within twelve to twenty-four hours after the donor's death. It does not have to be removed in a sterile operating room. Skin bank technicians go wherever the body is, such as the hospital morgue or the funeral home.

After the skin is shaved, washed with an antiseptic, and lubricated with mineral oil, it is removed from the donor using an electric instrument called a **dermatome.** The dermatome has a sharp vibrating blade, like a razor blade, that can be adjusted to remove different thicknesses. The dermatome shaves off long strips of skin, 3 or 4 inches (7.5 to 10 cm) wide and less than a millimeter thick—slightly thinner than a credit card. The thin outer layer, called the **epidermis,** is removed as well as part of the thicker underlying layer, called the **dermis.** The skin is usually taken from areas normally covered by clothing so as not to disfigure the donor. As each strip of skin is removed it is placed in a separate jar containing a sterile nutrient. These jars are packed in ice for their trip to the skin bank.

Donor skin is most effective when it is removed soon after the donor's death and grafted immediately onto the burn patient. Usually, however, the timing doesn't work out this well, so the skin must be stored. It can be kept in the refrigerator for several days or frozen for longer periods of time.

Skin that is to be frozen is first soaked in a special solution that protects the cells from damage during the freezing process. Then the strips are cut to a uniform size, placed between two pieces of gauze, and sealed in a plastic packet. A tiny piece of each strip is saved for testing. Skin from one donor can make five or six dozen packets of skin.

CROSS SECTION OF SKIN

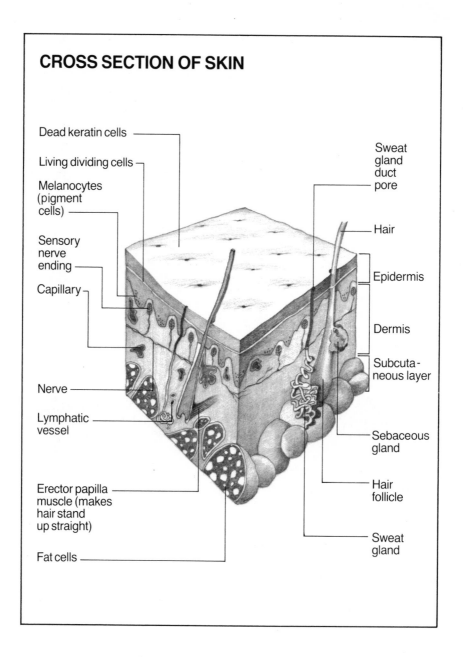

Dead keratin cells

Living dividing cells

Melanocytes (pigment cells)

Sensory nerve ending

Capillary

Nerve

Lymphatic vessel

Erector papilla muscle (makes hair stand up straight)

Fat cells

Sweat gland duct pore

Hair

Epidermis

Dermis

Subcuta-neous layer

Sebaceous gland

Hair follicle

Sweat gland

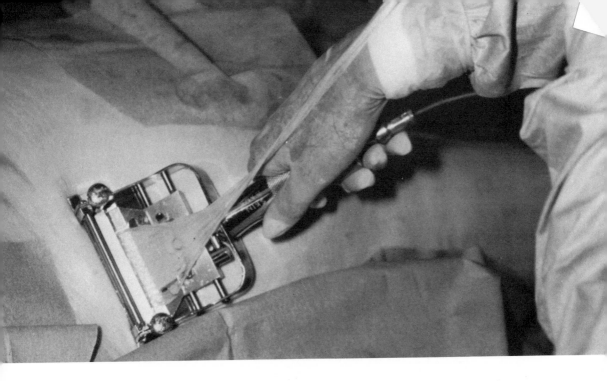

Above: *a dermatone is used to remove thin strips of skin from the donor's body.* Below: *after being soaked in a special solution, the strips of skin are placed between two pieces of gauze.*

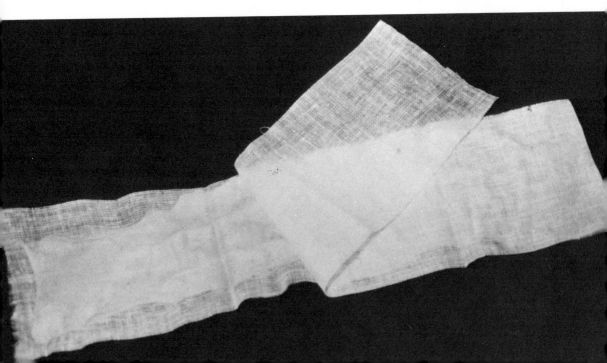

Skin bank equipment includes a computer attached to a freezing chamber (left) and a liquid nitrogen freezer (center), which provides for long-term storage of skin.

Skin must be frozen slowly to keep the cells from being destroyed. The best freezers use liquid nitrogen and are controlled by computers to lower the temperature at a slow, steady rate. Once the skin reaches −70 degrees Celsius (−94° F), the packets can be transferred to a storage freezer and kept indefinitely.

When skin is needed for grafting, the packets are thawed rapidly in warm water. Because the skin is so thin, it only takes fifteen to thirty seconds to thaw each packet. Then the skin is rinsed to remove the freezing solution.

Donor skin is laid over the burned areas of a patient and held in place with adhesive strips and spray adhesive. It can also be covered with sterilized nylon netting secured by surgical staples.

The gauze-covered strips of skin are placed in packets, then frozen.

When skin grafts are done on limbs, those limbs must not be moved for a few days to give the skin a chance to take hold.

When there are shortages, skin can be made to stretch across a larger area. This is done by laying each strip on a piece of plastic and putting it through a "mesher." This machine cuts tiny slits in the skin so that when it is pulled wide it resembles a fishnet. Sometimes a strip of the patient's skin is cut into a wide mesh and laid over the burn. Then it is covered with donor skin that has been cut into a tighter mesh. The patient's own skin grows and slowly fills in the spaces. By the time the donor skin is rejected, the patient's new skin is ready to take over.

Donor skin is not expected to last. It is merely a temporary solution until grafts can be made using the patient's own skin. Recovering skin from a living person is similar to mowing a lawn. Doctors must wait until new skin grows back before they can collect more. In the meantime, the burned areas can be covered with cadaver skin.

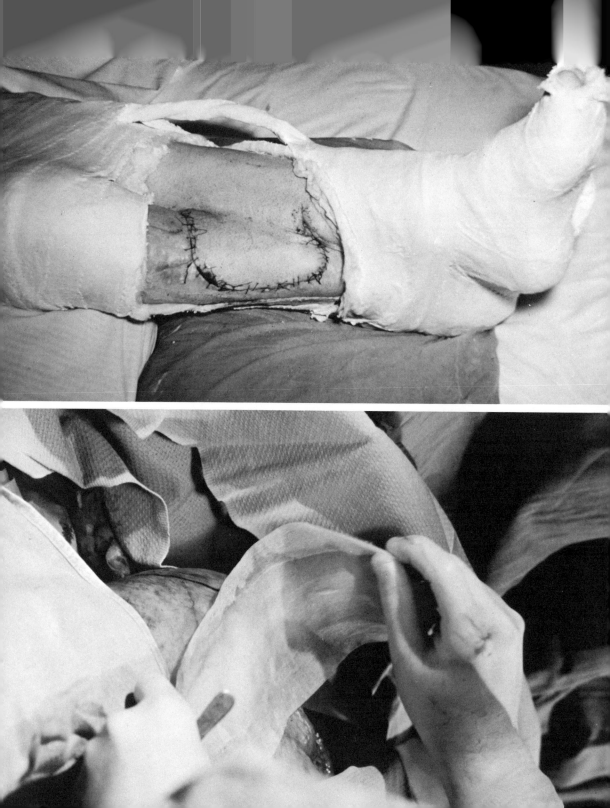

The first graft of donor skin usually lasts up to five weeks because the patient's severe burns have depressed his or her immune system. Eventually, the body becomes well enough to recognize that the donor skin is a foreign body and rejects it. An antirejection drug, such as cyclosporine, can be used to make the donor graft last longer.

Of the two million Americans burned each year, only the most serious need donor skin, but they need a lot of it. One burn patient normally needs skin from several donors. Most skin banks cannot keep up with the demand. Their main problem is a lack of donors. Only one or two percent of the people who die in the United States donate their skin. These are mainly people who have agreed to donate whatever is needed. More people would probably donate skin at death if they were aware of its importance in treating burns.

Scientists are constantly trying to find better ways to provide skin for severely burned patients. Researchers in Boston have developed an artificial skin by combining cowhide, shark cartilage, and plastic. It is made to resemble human skin as much as possible. However, this artificial skin has not yet proven to be as successful as the patient's own skin or even cadaver skin.

A more promising development involves growing skin in laboratories. A small piece of a patient's skin is placed in a special tissue culture. Within weeks a piece of skin the size of a dime can grow into enough skin to cover an entire arm. Since this skin is

Above: *a leg skin graft using the patient's own skin.* Below: *donor skin is laid over the open wound of a burn victim. Eventually, the patient's own skin grows in to replace it.*

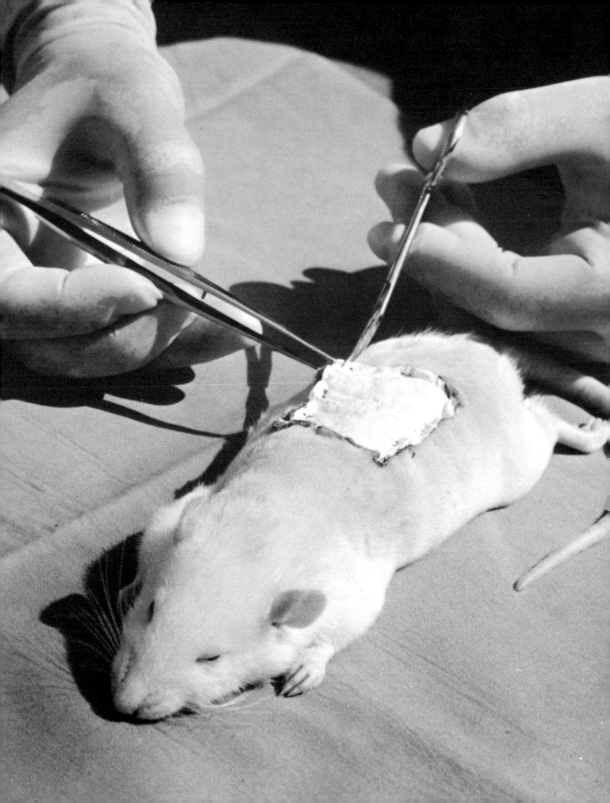

made from the patient's own cells it is not rejected. The drawback is that only the outer epidermis can be grown. The dermis, the part of the skin containing the blood vessels and nerves, cannot be grown. The epidermis alone can be used for burn victims' faces, but without the dermis underneath, the epidermis will not be as durable as normal skin grafts. Even many patients who are treated with this new skin must rely on skin from the skin bank while they are waiting for their "test tube" skin to grow.

Most skin from skin banks is used for burn patients, but it can also help those suffering from large open wounds. The donor skin closes the wound, at least temporarily, keeping infection out and reducing the pain. Donor skin can also be used as a test to see if the wound is ready to take a graft of the patient's own skin. This avoids wasting the patient's skin with repeated grafts.

Burns are perhaps the most painful and most disfiguring of any bodily injury. Whether a burn victim receives skin grafts from his or her own body or from a donor, the body will still be badly scarred. Without skin from skin banks, many burn victims would suffer through a much longer and more painful healing process. Many of them would not survive at all.

Many researchers have experimented with different types of artificial skin.

EIGHT

DONOR BANKRUPTCY

Most donor banks agree that there are never enough donors. They all face shortages, some more than others. Blood banks are better off than most. Although they can always use more donors, they are not usually hampered by the critical shortages facing most organ and tissue banks.

Even with more people today donating organs when they die, the gap continues to widen between the number of organs available and the number needed. This is because of the remarkable progress in transplant medicine in recent years. Because of improved surgical techniques, better antirejection drugs, and the ability to diagnose rejection earlier, more people are becoming candidates for transplants. New transplant centers are springing up all over the country, and all of them need organs and tissues.

In the United States each year, an estimated 20,000 people die in ways that would make them suitable organ donors. These are usually young or middle-aged people who die suddenly from accidents or strokes. Many of them die in hospitals while being maintained on life-support systems, which qualifies them as donors of vital organs. Even those who cannot donate hearts, livers, and kidneys would make acceptable donors for corneas, skin, and bones. Yet out of all these deaths, only a small percentage result in any donated organ or tissue.

The critical shortage is felt most by the thousands of people waiting for needed organs. A third of those needing heart transplants die before a suitable organ becomes available. Many children who need livers never survive the wait. The American Council on Transplantation (ACT) estimates that in 1985, 9,800 people were waiting for kidney transplants, 4,000 needed corneas, 300 needed hearts, 400 needed livers, and 100 needed pancreases. These figures don't include those needing grafts of bone or skin. The need for organs for infants and children is even more critical. As a last resort, California heart surgeons gave "Baby Faye" the heart of a baboon because no human heart of her size was available. Baby Faye did not survive.

Why don't more people donate their organs and tissues? Polls have shown that most people approve of human transplants and would be willing to donate the organs of a loved one if that person had mentioned organ donation before death. But when it comes to donating their own organs, the numbers drop considerably. Most people simply don't want to think about their own death, much less make plans for their body after they die.

People have many concerns about donating their own organs or those of a loved one who has just died and not left any instructions on organ donation. Some are afraid the removal will leave the body disfigured. This does not happen. Organs and tissues are removed from the donor as carefully as they would be removed from a living person. All the incisions are covered by clothing during the funeral. Those viewing the donor in an open casket will not be able to tell that anything has been removed.

Some people are afraid that if the doctors know they have agreed to donate their organs, they won't work as hard to save their lives. Or they are afraid the doctors will start removing the organs before the donor is actually dead. Both of these fears are unfounded. The first priority of every doctor is to give patients the best care possible. It is only after all hope is gone and after extensive tests have been done that the patient is declared brain dead. Only then can the process of organ and tissue donation begin. To avoid any conflict of interest, doctors who take care of the donor before death never participate in removing the organs or in the transplant surgery.

Some families have trouble accepting brain death. They can see their loved one breathing. They can feel the heart beating and the warmth of the skin. They don't understand how the person can look so alive and still be dead. But a person who is brain dead cannot function at all without the respirator; the person is no different than a patient who is more obviously dead. Specific tests are performed before the patient is declared brain dead. This includes taking the patient off the respirator to see if he or she can breathe independently.

Some people worry that their religion might disapprove of organ donation. However, all the major religions support organ donation. Some even consider it a moral obligation to give the gift of life to another. Any doubts can be cleared up by talking to a member of the clergy.

By far the biggest reason more organs are not donated is that most families are never asked. Doctors and nurses are often uncomfortable discussing organ donation with a grief-stricken family. Yet it has been shown that over 60 percent of the families who were asked agreed to it. Most appreciated the opportunity to have something positive come out of their tragedy.

To help provide the needed organs for transplantation the Uniform Anatomical Gift Act was adopted in the early 1970s. This act makes it possible for adults to voluntarily donate some or all of their organs when they die. They only need to complete a uniform donor card and have it signed by two witnesses. This card is carried in the person's wallet, where it can be found by hospital personnel in case of accidental death. Many states have made this process easier by including a similar form on the back of the driver's license. If no card is found, the donor's next of kin must give permission for the donation. In fact, the donor's family is always consulted before organs are removed even when a donor card is present.

Although the idea of carrying a donor card is good, it has not been as successful as donor banks had hoped. Most adults know about the cards, but less than 20 percent have signed one. Among actual organ donors, only 3 percent had a donor card with them when they died. In many cases a victim's card was not found in time, so the organs were not donated according to the person's wishes.

New laws are being passed in some states to ease the problem of shortages. Some have adopted the law of "presumed consent," but only pertaining to corneas. This law allows corneas to be removed from anyone sent to the medical examiner unless someone in the family objects. Several European countries have expanded the practice of presumed consent to cover all organs. This would be one possible solution to the shortage of organs in the United States, but not one the public seems eager to accept.

Some people feel that more organs would be donated if the donor's families were paid for the organs. However, this solution would create a multitude of legal and ethical problems. It could encourage corruption and unfair distribution of organs. There is now a federal law prohibiting the sale of organs.

Perhaps the best solution is the practice of "required request." Since it has been shown that most families agree to donate organs if they are asked, ways must be found to give more families this option. As said earlier, most doctors and nurses never mention organ donation to potential donors or their families for various reasons. Some are uncomfortable discussing the subject. Others are worried about future legal problems. Still others have not been trained to recognize potential donors or don't know who to contact to get the procedure started. To solve this problem, some states are passing laws that require someone on the hospital staff to discuss organ donation with the family of every potential donor.

If all states followed the practice of required request, the topic of organ donation would become routine. Families would know ahead of time that they would be asked to make this decision and could discuss it before a death actually occurred. Decisions concerning the donation of organs could become as routine as decisions concerning funeral and burial arrangements.

Donating the organs of a loved one does not cause any added work or expense on the part of the donor's family. Once they have signed the consent form, everything is handled by the donor banks or hospital. Donor families are never billed for expenses related to a donation. Since the organs are removed soon after death, the process will not interfere with funeral plans.

It is easy to make sure that your organs will be donated in the unlikely event that something should happen to you. You may obtain a uniform donor card from any donor bank listed in your telephone book or from the organizations listed at the end of this book. You may specify on the card whether you want to donate only certain organs or anything that is needed. The card must be signed by two witnesses. If you are under eighteen years of age, your parents must witness the card for you.

Signing a donor card isn't enough. You must make sure the rest of your family knows your wishes. In the confusion of an

The next of kin must always sign a consent form, such as this one, for organ donation, even if you have signed a donor card.

MARYLAND ORGAN PROCUREMENT CENTER, INC.
MARYLAND TISSUE BANK & LABORATORY, INC.
(301) 528-3626

CONSENT FORM FOR THE

GIFT OF BODY, ORGAN AND / OR TISSUE

DATE _____
                   a.m.
TIME _____ p.m.

In accordance with the Maryland Anatomical Gift Act, I hereby give to the appropriate organ and tissue procurement agency (agencies):

☐ the body   ☐ any needed organs or tissues   ☐ tissue - skin   ☐ the following organs or tissues, _____

of the decedent, _____ , for the

following purposes:

       ☐   any purpose authorized by law

       ☐   transplantation

       ☐   therapy

       ☐   medical research and education.

In documenting this anatomical gift, I certify that in relationship to the decedent I am a: ☐ surviving spouse; ☐ adult son or daughter; ☐ parent; ☐ adult brother or sister; ☐ person authorized or obligated to dispose of the decedent's body. I further certify that, to the best of my knowledge, I am not aware of any controversy among decedent's next of kin regarding the making of this anatomical gift.

I have read and fully understand this document.

Signed _____

Witness _____   Date _____

Witness _____   Date _____

emergency, donor cards are often not found in time. Even if you have signed a card, no organs will be removed without your family's permission. Knowing how you feel makes their decision easier. If for some reason you change your mind about donating, all you have to do is tear up your card and tell your family.

People who are organ donors have already died. Nothing more can be done for them. Yet even in their death they can make a great contribution. The gifts from only one donor could give life to someone whose heart is failing, to another whose liver has ceased to function, and another whose pancreas has stopped producing needed insulin. That same donor can free two people from the agonizing hours spent each week on kidney dialysis machines. Two people with limited sight would be able to see the world more clearly. That's seven lives that could be saved or improved by only one donor, and that doesn't include perhaps twenty or more who could benefit from donations of skin and bones.

Most of us will never have the opportunity to become heroes while we are alive. Few of us will ever rescue a drowning child or pull someone from the flames of a burning building. Many of us wouldn't even try these rescues because of the risk to our own lives. But thousands of people every year become heroes by saving lives after they die. Death marks the end of one life, but organ donation marks the continuation of many others.

FOR MORE INFORMATION

AMERICAN ASSOCIATION OF BLOOD BANKS
1117 North 19th Street, Suite 600
Arlington, Virginia 22209

AMERICAN ASSOCIATION OF TISSUE BANKS
1117 North 19th Street, Suite 402
Arlington, Virginia 22209

AMERICAN COUNCIL ON TRANSPLANTATION
4701 Willard Avenue, Suite 222
Chevy Chase, Maryland 20815

AMERICAN LIVER FOUNDATION
998 Pompton Avenue
Cedar Grove, New Jersey 07009

EYE BANK ASSOCIATION OF AMERICA
1511 K Street, N.W.
Suite 830
Washington, D.C. 20005-1401

THE LIVING BANK
P.O. Box 6725
Houston, Texas 77265

NATIONAL KIDNEY FOUNDATION
Two Park Avenue
New York, New York 10016

NATIONAL TEMPORAL BONE BANKS PROGRAM
243 Charles Street
Boston, Massachusetts 02114

GLOSSARY

ANTIBODIES—special protein molecules in the blood manufactured to help neutralize or destroy foreign substances or antigens that have gained entry into the body.

ANTIGEN—any substance that, when it gets into the body, can stimulate the production of antibodies.

APHERESIS—a process whereby blood is separated to remove a particular component, such as platelets or plasma, with the rest of the blood being returned to the donor.

BIOPSY—the removal of a small piece of living tissue from an organ or other part of the body for microscopic examination.

BRAIN DEATH—an irreversible form of unconsciousness characterized by a complete loss of brain function.

CADAVER—a dead body used for dissection, study, or as a source of transplantable organs and tissues.

CELL—the smallest unit capable of independent life. All living things are made up of different types of cells.

CENTRIFUGE—a device for separating components of different densities contained in liquid by spinning them at high speeds. In blood banking it is used to separate whole blood into its components.

CORNEA—the curved transparent tissue covering the iris and pupil on the outside of the eye.

CYCLOSPORINE—an antirejection drug that suppresses the specific cells that attack a transplanted organ.

CYTOPLASM—a jellylike substance that makes up the entire cell except for the nucleus.

DERMATOME—an instrument for cutting thin layers of skin for grafts.

DERMIS—the bottom layer of skin lying beneath the epidermis that contains blood vessels, hair roots, glands, elastic fibers, and fat.

DIALYSIS—the process of diffusing blood across a semipermeable membrane to remove liquid and chemicals that the kidneys would normally remove if they were present and functioning.

DONOR—a human or animal that gives away living tissue to be used by another, such as blood for transfusion or organs for transplantation.

EPIDERMIS—the top layer of skin; contains no blood vessels.

NUCLEUS—a structure within a cell that controls the cell's activities and contains the cell's hereditary material.

ORGAN—a group of tissues that work together to perform a certain function within the body.

PERFUSION PUMP—a machine used to circulate nutrients and oxygen through kidneys that have been removed from a donor for transplantation.

PLASMA—the liquid part of the blood; contains no cells.

PLATELETS—tiny, colorless structures in the blood that help to initiate blood clotting.

RECIPIENT—a person who receives an organ or tissue from a donor through transplantation or transfusion.

RED BLOOD CELLS—cells in the blood that carry oxygen from the lungs to the body's cells and bring carbon dioxide back to the lungs.

REJECTION—a response by the immune system to an organism or substance that the system recognizes as foreign, including transplanted organs and tissues.

RESPIRATOR—a mechanical breathing device for patients who are unable to breathe on their own.

SKIN GRAFT—a piece of skin that is taken from one area of a patient's body or from a donor's body and used to replace skin in another area.

SLIT LAMP—an instrument for examining parts of the eye; a high-intensity beam of light is projected through the slit, allowing the illuminated part to be examined through a magnifying lens.

SYSTEM—a group of organs that work together to carry on certain vital functions of the body.

TISSUE—a group of the same kinds of cells that work together to do a certain job.

TISSUE TYPING—a series of tests to evaluate the compatibility of donor and recipient tissue. Tissue typing is done to lessen the chances of rejection.

TRANSFUSION—the introduction into the bloodstream of whole blood or blood components.

TREPHINE—an instrument used to cut a small circle of cornea for removal or transplantation.

INDEX

ABOUT
THE AUTHOR

Sally Lee is a writer and former special education teacher. She has written numerous stories and articles for various young reader publications, including *Cricket, Teen,* and *Highlights for Children.* This is her first book.

Mrs. Lee lives in San Antonio, Texas, with her husband Stephen, who is a petroleum engineer, and her two children, Michael and Tracy.